The Girl Who Lives

on the Rainbow

by Jamie Lewis

Illustrated by Darya Shch

The Girl Who Lives on The Rainbow © 2017 Jamie Lewis

Illustrations by Darya Shch

ISBN-13: 978-0-9989227-0-6

ISBN-10 0-9989227-0-6

This book is dedicated to Clint, Wally, Daisy, Mindy, Mandy and Decker.
You are all forever in my heart.

The Girl Who Lives on the Rainbow

Ever since she could remember Grace loved animals. It didn't matter if they were big or small, furry or feathery, young or old. There was something magical and special about each and every animal that she met.

Whenever Grace was outside playing and a dog walked by, she always stopped whatever she was doing and watched with delight. If she didn't already know the dog, she would ask his owner if it was ok to pet him. She learned the names of all of the dogs in the neighborhood. They were all perfect.

Even the shy dogs enjoyed being petted by her. They seemed to know that she loved them and would never hurt them. Every day she could count on seeing Buster and Peanut, two very cute little brown and white terrier mix dogs, along with Cookie and Coco, the silly Chihuahua brothers who lived down the street. There was also Rocky, a big German Shepherd who got his name because he liked to carry rocks in his mouth. They were just a few of the ones she knew by name.

If Grace was outside and saw a kitty strolling down the sidewalk or sitting in a yard, she would pause and quietly watch the kitty, following her every move. She knew that making too much noise or moving too fast would scare the kitty. She might run away from her and that's the last thing that Grace would want!

If the kitty looked friendly Grace would approach her speaking very softly.

If she seemed friendly and would like to be petted, Grace would reach down and pet the side of her head and ears. Often there would be a sweet little 'meow'. Grace was certain that the kitty was bidding a friendly 'hello, it's really nice to meet you'.

She knew the names of a few of the kitties in the neighborhood since they had collars with nametags on them. There was Mindy, Bella, Sugar, Princess and Quinn, just to name a few.

As the years went by and Grace grew up, all of the dogs and cats got a little older too, as they tend to do in this world.

Grace noticed that her animal friends seemed to be slowing down. Buster and Peanut weren't playing as often as they used to. They weren't outside taking as many walks or going on as many adventures as before.

Then one day she noticed that, one by one, day-by-day, week-by-week, her animal friends seemed to begin to disappear. She became sad at the thought of losing her friends. There were many new animals of course. But she loved the animals that grew up with her so much. There was no way that they could really disappear. She knew this could not be the case. Love never dies. She was quite sure of that.

But where could they have gone? Could she go there too?

One summer day after a rainstorm, a giant and perfectly formed rainbow appeared in the sky. The sun was shining and the sky was filled with soft puffy clouds that looked like bunches of cotton balls floating in the air. When she looked to the East, she saw the most beautiful rainbow she had ever seen.

Grace walked across the field nearby to see if she could get closer. The rainbow got bigger and bigger the closer she got. The colors became more vibrant and beautiful. When she looked up into the rainbow she saw that there was something sparkling and twinkling inside of it.

The red part of the rainbow had sparkles twinkling off and on like magic rubies. Bright orange sparkles lit up the orange stripe and spilled over into the sunshiny yellow. The yellow was as bright and bold as the sun. All of its light was made of yellow sparkles that twinkled like diamonds.

This rainbow was alive!

The green part of the rainbow felt like summer itself and shone like satin. This summer green began to gently blend into the softest baby blue she had ever seen.

Blue sparkles flowed out from the rainbow and led the way into the most majestic colors of all: The royal purple and the deep violet blue shade of indigo. Like taking a breath of fresh air, she could breathe in the colors as she looked at them.

When she reached these last two colors of the rainbow, something magical happened. She reached up to touch the colors and a beautiful bridge appeared. It led up into the very heart of the rainbow.

Grace carefully stepped onto the bridge and followed it up and up, higher and higher she went.

When she reached the top, she stopped and gazed out into the lovely colors before her. On the other side of this bridge was a meadow. A meadow just like the field near her home. Except this meadow had something extra special about it.

It was filled with all of the animals that she had ever known that used to live on earth. Mystery solved! So this is where they had all gone!

They were running and playing again. Some (especially the cats) were just relaxing and basking in the sunshine, which somehow seemed warmer and brighter here.

Where was she? Was this Heaven?

Grace then realized that this magical place was perfect.

Yes. It was Heaven.

Everything that anyone needed to live a full and happy life was always provided. Even Grace's favorite food! All she had to do was reach up into a cloud, and the cloud became her favorite flavor of cotton candy. A little pull. ...and yum! Another gentle tug on a cloud and, voila! There was a piece of Angel Food Cake!

The animals had plenty of fresh air and sunshine. A beautiful stream ran through the patch of woods on the far side of the meadow. There was shelter and food for everyone. Then, she remembered! She realized that this *was* her real home. She actually *did* live here! She was *from* here! This was where she belonged and she had finally returned.

She walked around getting reacquainted with all of her friends. It was so wonderful seeing them again. There was Buster, the dog who lived down the street from her when she was in 3rd grade! Next over the bridge came Princess, the beautiful longhaired cat that used to live next door to her Grandma!

Grace began meeting new animals too. As she was standing there looking out over the meadow, she turned to look back over the bridge she had walked across. To her surprise and delight, two majestic horses appeared followed closely behind by two little dogs.

They all greeted her and thanked her for being there to welcome them. They knew that she would help take care of them until their human parents arrived.

Over the years Grace made many trips back and forth across the rainbow bridge to tell the people on Earth that their pets were safe, happy and well cared for on the other side and were waiting patiently. She always liked visiting with the animals that still lived on earth. There were always so many new ones to meet and get to know.

Grace realized that all animals had always known about the Rainbow Bridge. They were glad that she had remembered it too and that it would always be there for them too, when they needed it.

Over the next days, weeks, months and years, Grace met many new arrivals over the Rainbow Bridge. There were bunnies, goats, birds, cows, and hamsters. There were more animals than she could ever count. It was the perfect place that she had always imagined existed when she was on Earth.

Everyone was happy and healthy. Everyone got along and was kind to every species. There was plenty of fresh food and water and treats for everyone.

Time passed but no one ever got any older.
No one ever got sick. No one ever died.

Yes. This was Heaven. And Grace lived there
happily ever after surrounded by Love.

Rainbow Bridge

Just this side of Heaven is a place called Rainbow Bridge. When an animal dies that has been especially close to someone here, that pet goes to Rainbow Bridge. There are meadows and hills for all of our special friends so they can run and play together. There is plenty of food, water and sunshine, and our friends are warm and comfortable. All the animals who had been ill and old are restored to health and vigor. Those who were hurt or maimed are made whole and strong again, just as we remember them in our dreams of days and times gone by. The animals are happy and content, except for one small thing; they each miss someone very special to them, who had to be left behind.

They all run and play together, but the day comes when one suddenly stops and looks into the distance. His bright eyes are intent. His eager body quivers. Suddenly he begins to run from the group, flying over green grass, his legs carrying him faster and faster...

You have been spotted, and when you and your special friend finally meet, you cling together in joyous reunion, never to be parted again. The happy kisses rain upon your face; your hands again caress the beloved head, and you look once more into the trusting eyes of your pet, so long gone from your life but never absent from your heart. Then you cross Rainbow Bridge together...
-Author Unknown

Jamie Lewis lives in California with her husband, 2 dogs, 4 cats, and 2 goats. When she is not taking care of the fur kids, she is teaching music to students of all ages. She plays keyboards and sings in a Top 40 band.

www.ingramcontent.com/pod-product-compliance
Lightning Source LLC
Chambersburg PA
CBHW041222040426
42443CB00002B/58